**The Creation Se**
**A Bible-based Re**

CW00348480

# Birds

# Carole Leah
# and Sharon Rentta

## NOTE TO PARENTS AND TEACHERS

The Creation Series consists of eight books based on the Genesis account in the Bible. This is the fifth book of the series and has been written from a Christian viewpoint. It is intended to be read *to* 3-4 year olds. The series prepares children to read and extend their vocabulary. In this book children can develop and practise preparatory skills for reading as well as appreciate God's care.

## BIBLE REFERENCES

All Bible references are in bold throughout and are as follows: p10 Genesis 1:21

## ENCOURAGE CHILDREN TO:

* Talk about the illustrations and retell the story in their own words.
* Look out for different birds and name some.
* Draw their own picture of their favourite bird.
* Memorise the Bible verse and its reference (see page 24).
* Learn about the different parts of a bird from looking at a real bird - its tail, head, beak, wings, legs, feet.
* Talk about the homes that birds make for their young and the different eggs that birds lay. (See pages 12-13).
* Ensure that the children know the meaning of all these words: *heaven* (God's home); *hooting* (a crying noise, twit-twoo); *screech* (a sudden cry, a yell); *stare* (to look at for a long time); *strut* (to walk slowly with the head held high); *sweetly* (softly, beautifully); *waddle* (walking from side to side with a little step).

Carole Leah became a Christian at a youth camp when she was seventeen years old while reading a Gideon New Testament. She felt called to write these books so that young children would learn the truth about God while also developing their reading and vocabulary skills. Several people have worked alongside Carole as she wrote this material but she would like to especially dedicate these books to the memory of her dear friend Ruth Martin who gave so much support.

All scripture quotations in this publication are from the Good News Translation in Today's English Version - Second Edition Copyright © 1992 by American Bible Society. Used by Permission.
Text copyright © Carole Leah. Illustrations copyright © Sharon Rentta
ISBN: 978-1-84550-533-2 Published by Christian Focus Publications, Geanies House, Fearn, Tain, Ross-shire, IV20 1TW, Scotland, U.K.
www.christianfocus.com

Todd, Daniel and Joy are on a farm.
See what they are doing in this book!

The children are looking at some birds.
Todd is feeding a hen and her chicks.

---

Look for the budgerigars (budgies)!

Can you find more than 10
pictures of budgerigars in this book?

Did you know that a daddy budgerigar has
a blue patch above his beak and a mummy
budgerigar has a brown patch above her beak?

In the beginning

there were no birds in the sky.

God spoke and

made birds out of soil from the ground.

Most birds could fly in the sky.

God made little birds and big birds.

He created birds that sing sweetly.

He made birds that screech loudly.

He created birds that waddle along.

He made birds that fly high.

God blessed all the birds.

He gave the birds grass and

leafy plants to eat.

**...God was pleased with what he saw.**

God told the birds to have many young ones.

13

Now, Daniel likes to talk to

the pretty parrots that talk back to him.

Now, Joy likes to copy

the beautiful peacocks that strut along.

Now, Todd likes to copy

the hooting owls that sit and stare.

God cares for all the different birds.

He even knows when

one little bird falls to the ground.

Daniel, Todd and Joy are happy.

They know that God cares for them even

more than he cares for all the birds.

God cares for us in a special way, too!

Jesus said... **'Look at the birds:**

**...your Father in heaven**

**takes care of them!...'**

Matthew, chapter 6, verse 26